55 Arthritis Meal Recipes to Help Reduce Pain and Discomfort:

Natural Meal Remedies for Arthritis That Work

By

Joe Correa CSN

COPYRIGHT

© 2016 Live Stronger Faster Inc.

All rights reserved

Reproduction or translation of any part of this work beyond that permitted by section 107 or 108 of the 1976 United States Copyright Act without the permission of the copyright owner is unlawful.

This publication is designed to provide accurate and authoritative information in regard to the subject matter covered. It is sold with the understanding that neither the author nor the publisher is engaged in rendering medical advice. If medical advice or assistance is needed, consult with a doctor. This book is considered a guide and should not be used in any way detrimental to your health. Consult with a physician before starting this nutritional plan to make sure it's right for you.

ACKNOWLEDGEMENTS

This book is dedicated to my friends and family that have had mild or serious illnesses so that you may find a solution and make the necessary changes in your life.

55 Arthritis Meal Recipes to Help Reduce Pain and Discomfort:

Natural Meal Remedies for Arthritis That Work

By

Joe Correa CSN

CONTENTS

Copyright

Acknowledgements

About The Author

Introduction

55 Arthritis Meal Recipes to Help Reduce Pain and Discomfort: Natural Meal Remedies for Arthritis That Work

Additional Titles from This Author

ABOUT THE AUTHOR

After years of Research, I honestly believe in the positive effects that proper nutrition can have over the body and mind. My knowledge and experience has helped me live healthier throughout the years and which I have shared with family and friends. The more you know about eating and drinking healthier, the sooner you will want to change your life and eating habits.

Nutrition is a key part in the process of being healthy and living longer so get started today. The first step is the most important and the most significant.

INTRODUCTION

55 Arthritis Meal Recipes to Help Reduce Pain and Discomfort: Natural Meal Remedies for Arthritis That Work

By Joe Correa CSN

There are 100 million forms of arthritis and the most common one is osteoarthritis, as a result of a trauma, infection of the joint or age. In order to prevent arthritis or to reduce its effects, a healthy diet is required. A lot of fruits, vegetables, fat in fish and nuts. These foods represent an amazing army of inflammation fighters. Moreover, your weight will be under control: for every one pound of weight you lose, the load on your knee joint will be reduced by 4 pounds.

It is important to keep in mind that there is no magic trick to get rid of arthritis, but a healthy diet will certainly help fight inflammation and joint pain, strenghten bones and boost your immune system.

Many of these ingredients recommended for people with arthritis can be found in Mediterranean diets, that contain olive oil, fish and vegetables. Also, Vitamin C needs to be included in your diet. The reason for this is because the antioxidants found in this vitamin may slow down the progression of osteoarthritis. You can get this vitamin from strawberries, pineapples, kiwi, avocado, oranges or apples.

55 ARTHRITIS MEAL RECIPES TO HELP REDUCE PAIN AND DISCOMFORT: NATURAL MEAL REMEDIES FOR ARTHRITIS THAT WORK

1. **Super Broccoli Power**

Description:
Broccoli is very rich in vitamins K, C, and calcium, which is known for its bone-building benefits.

Ingredients:

- 2 cups broccoli florets
- 1 yellow bell pepper, sliced
- 2 teaspoons chili powder
- 1 teaspoon garlic powder
- salt and pepper to taste
- 1 tablespoon extra-virgin olive oil

How to prepare:

- Preheat an oven to 400 degrees F (200 degrees C).
- Combine the broccoli and bell pepper in a bowl. Sprinkle, chili powder, garlic powder, salt, and pepper over the vegetables; drizzle with the olive oil and toss to coat. Spread the vegetables into a shallow baking dish.

- Bake in the preheated oven until the vegetables are tender and beginning to brown, 15 to 20 minutes.

Nutritional facts:

Calories: 69kcal, Fat: 3.9g, Carbs: 8g, Protein: 2.1g, Sodium: 815mg

2. Crunchy Eggplant Delight

Description:
Nightshade vegetables, including eggplant, are disease-fighting powerhouses that give the maximum nutrition for a small number of calories.

Ingredients:

- eggplant, sliced into strips
- 1/2 cup soft bread crumbs
- 1/8 cup grated Romano cheese
- 1 clove garlic, chopped
- 2 sprigs fresh parsley, chopped
- 1/2 teaspoon dried oregano
- salt and pepper to taste

How to prepare:

- Preheat oven to 400 degrees F (200 degrees C).
- Cut eggplant strips in half. Lay strips on a baking sheet.
- In a small bowl combine bread crumbs, Romano cheese, garlic, parsley, oregano, salt and pepper. Sprinkle over eggplant strips and drizzle with oil.
- Bake in preheated oven for 25 minutes

Nutritional facts:
Calories: 169kcal, Fat: 8.9g, Carbs: 19g, Sodium: 155mg

3. Healthberries

Description:

Recent clinical studies have shown that diets containing an abundance of flavonoids (a broad class of plant pigments) are associated with reduced levels of inflammation. These natural compounds are found especially in strawberries

Ingredients:

- 2 bunches spinach
- 4 cups sliced strawberries
- 1/2 cup vegetable oil
- 1/4 cup white wine vinegar
- 1/2 cup white sugar
- 1/4 teaspoon paprika
- 2 tablespoons sesame seeds
- 1 tablespoon poppy seeds

How to prepare:

- In a large bowl, toss together the spinach and strawberries.
- Whisk together the oil, vinegar, sugar, paprika, sesame seeds, and poppy seeds. Pour over the spinach and strawberries.

Nutritional facts:
Calories: 255kcal, Fat: 16g, Carbs: 22.8g, Sodium: 69mg

4. Lemon Broccolini

Description:

A broccoli lovers delight with a sweet-and-sour taste! Broccoli is abundant in vitamin K, which in high amounts may slow the progression of osteoarthritis.

Ingredients:

- 1 head fresh broccoli, cut into florets
- 1 tablespoon olive oil
- 2 tablespoons lemon juice
- 1 teaspoon lemon zest
- 1/4 cup blanched slivered almonds

How to prepare:

- Steam or boil broccoli until tender, approximately 4 to 8 minutes. Drain.
- In a small saucepan, melt olive oil over medium low heat. Remove from heat.
- Stir in lemon juice. lemon zest, and almonds. Pour over hot broccoli, and serve.

Nutritional facts:
Calories: 170 kcal, Fat: 15.2g, Carbs: 7g, Protein: 3.7g, Sodium: 107mg, Cholesterol: 31mg

5. Easy Flave Apples

Description:
Research suggests that eating some apple on a daily basis might lower levels of cholesterol, a key marker of inflammation in the blood. "An apple a day keeps the doctor away".

Ingredients:

- 2 apples, diced
- 1 teaspoon white sugar
- 1/2 teaspoon ground cinnamon

How to prepare:

- Place apples in a microwave-safe bowl; heat in microwave for 30 seconds. Sprinkle sugar and cinnamon over apples and stir to coat.
- Heat apples into the microwave until soft and warm, about 1 minute more.

Nutritional facts:
Calories: 255kcal, Fat: 16g, Carbs: 22.8g, Sodium: 69mg

6. Lemon Trout

Description:

One way to calm inflammation is with medicine your doctor prescribes. Another way is to add a few key anti-inflammatory foods to your diet. Among the most potent edible inflammation fighters are essential fatty acids called omega-3s – particularly the kinds of fatty acids found in trout.

Ingredients:

- 4 cups all-purpose flour
- 2 tablespoons lemon pepper
- 1/2 tablespoon salt
- 1/2 teaspoon dried thyme
- 1/2 teaspoon cayenne pepper
- 1 teaspoon onion powder
- 1/4 cup grated lemon zest, divided
- 4 (6 ounce) fillets rainbow trout
- 1 lemon cut in wedges
- 1/2 cup lemon juice
- 1/2 cup extra-virgin olive oil

How to prepare:

- In a large bowl, stir together the flour, lemon pepper, salt, thyme, cayenne and half of the lemon zest. Combine the lemon juice and

- remaining lemon zest in a shallow dish and soak fish fillets for about 1 minute.
- Heat oil in a large skillet over medium heat. Dip the trout fillets in the flour mixture so that both sides are coated. Shake off the excess and place fillets in the hot oil. Cook for 3 to 4 minutes on each side, until golden brown and fish can be flaked with a fork. Discard the leftover lemon juice.

Nutritional facts:
Calories: 979kcal, Fat: 40g, Carbs: 103g, Protein: 48.6g, Sodium: 2500mg

7. Salmons 'N' Lemons

Description:
Salmon helps reduce joint pain and stiffness as well as signs of inflammation in people with rheumatoid arthritis.

Ingredients:

- 1 (16 ounce) red salmon, drained and flaked
- 1 lemon, juiced
- 1/2 cup organic raisins
- 1 apple, cored and minced
- 1 1/2 stalks celery, chopped fine
- 1/3 cup mayonnaise, or to taste
- 1/4 teaspoon crushed red pepper flakes

How to prepare:

- Combine red salmon and lemon juice in a glass bowl; mix well.
- Stir in golden raisins, apple, celery, mayonnaise, and crushed red pepper flakes; mix thoroughly.

Nutritional facts:
Calories: 368kcal, Fat: 20.9g, Carbs: 21.2g, Protein: 25g, Sodium: 664mg

8. Salmon Asparagus Security

Description:

One cup of asparagus contains only 24 calories. It's also an excellent source of potassium, vitamin K, folic acid, vitamin C and A, riboflavin, thiamin, and vitamin B6.

Ingredients:

- 1 pound fresh asparagus, trimmed and cut into 1 inch pieces
- 1/2 cup pecans, broken into pieces
- 2 heads red leaf lettuce, rinsed and torn
- 1/2 cup green peas, thawed
- 1/4 pound organic smoked salmon, cut into 1 inch chunks
- 1/4 cup olive oil
- 2 tablespoons lemon juice
- 1 teaspoon Dijon mustard
- 1/2 teaspoon salt
- 1/4 teaspoon pepper

How to prepare:

- Bring a pot of water to a boil. Place asparagus in the pot, and cook 5 minutes, just until tender. Drain, and set aside.

- Place the pecans in a skillet over medium heat. Cook 5 minutes, stirring frequently, until lightly toasted.
- In a large bowl, toss together the asparagus, pecans, red leaf lettuce, peas, and salmon.
- In a separate bowl, mix the olive oil, lemon juice, Dijon mustard, salt, and pepper. Toss with the salad or serve on the side.

Nutritional facts:
Calories: 159kcal, Fat: 12.9g, Carbs: 7g, Protein: 6g, Sodium: 304mg

9. Canadian Style Salmon

Description:
Eating salmon once a week reduces risk of rheumatoid arthritis by half.

Ingredients:

- 1/4 cup maple syrup
- 1 tablespoon olive oil
- 1 clove garlic, minced
- 1/4 teaspoon garlic salt
- 1/8 teaspoon ground black pepper
- 1 pound salmon

How to prepare:

- In a small bowl, mix the maple syrup, garlic, garlic salt, and pepper.
- Place salmon in a shallow glass baking dish, and coat with the maple syrup mixture. Cover the dish, and marinate salmon in the refrigerator 30 minutes, turning once.
- Preheat oven to 400 degrees F (200 degrees C).
- Place the baking dish in the preheated oven, and bake salmon uncovered 20 minutes, or until easily flaked with a fork.

Nutritional facts:

Calories: 265kcal, Fat: 12g, Carbs: 14g, Protein: 23g, Sodium: 633mg

10. Neat Salmon

Description:

Quick, healthy dinner option. Low-calorie for weight loss. Wild-caught Sockeye salmon is a super food because of its omega-3 fatty acid content. Easy recipe for adding more Omega-3 EFAs in your diet.

Ingredients:

- 1 pound Wild-caught Salmon, cut into 4 filets
- 2 oranges, thinly sliced
- 3/4C fresh squeezed orange juice
- 2T fresh squeezed lime juice
- 2T virgin, unrefined coconut oil, melted or olive oil
- 1t lemon zest – dried or 1T fresh lemon zest
- 1T coconut or palm sugar or use raw honey or pure maple syrup
- coarsely ground salt
- 1/4t chipotle pepper or cayenne pepper or chili powder

How to prepare:

- preheat oven to 450º. Slice two oranges into very thin slices, discard ends, and set aside.
- Squeeze orange and lime with a citrus juicer. Measure out 1/4 cup fresh orange juice and 2

tablespoons fresh lime juice and add to a small glass bowl along with the lemon zest. Whisk in melted coconut oil or olive oil and sweetener of choice, along with salt and pepper.
- Line a baking sheet with parchment paper. Using a basting brush, brush one side of each of the salmon filets with the citrus mixture then arrange filets on top of parchment paper. Brush tops of salmon with the citrus mixture.

Nutritional facts:
Calories: 275, Fat: 18g, Carbs: 20g, Protein: 23g, Sodium: 215mg

11. Drunken Grapefruit Salad

Description:
Grapefruit is well known for its beneficial effects in patients with rheumatoid arthritis. Daily consumption of grapefruit has been associated with lowering of inflammation caused due to inflammatory diseases .

Ingredients:

- 8 cups refrigerated grapefruit, drained and juice reserved
- 1/4 cup white sugar
- 3 fluid ounces gin
- 8 leaves fresh mint, minced

How to prepare:

- Mix grapefruit, 1/2 cup reserved juice, and sugar in a bowl until sugar dissolves. Transfer grapefruit mixture to 8 serving cups; top each with about 1 teaspoon gin. Sprinkle minced mint over each cup. Garnish each cup with 1 mint leaf.

Nutritional facts:
Calories: 139kcal, Fat: 0.2g, Carbs: 28.6g, Protein: 1.4g, Sodium: 5mg

12. Grapefruit and its Friends

Description:
Grapefruit can be called as one of the Nature's medicine due to its tremendous health benefits. It is known to be beneficial for boosting the immune system. It is juicy, tangy and tart in taste and is known for its numerous health benefits. It is rich in antioxidants and various vitamins like Vitamin C, Vitamin A, Vitamin K, Vitamin D and Vitamin B complex.

Ingredients:

- 2 pink grapefruit, peeled and sectioned
- 1 large ripe avocado - peeled, pitted, and diced
- 1 cup alfalfa sprouts
- 1 lemon, juiced
- 3 tablespoons olive oil
- 1 pinch salt
- 1 pinch ground black pepper

How to prepare:

- Create 4 small salads with the fruits used
- Mix lemon juice, olive oil, salt, and black pepper in a small bowl; drizzle dressing over each salad.

Nutritional facts:
Calories: 277kcal, Fat: 20.7g, Carbs: 25.1g, Protein: 3.8g, Sodium: 7mg

13. Arthitis Buster

Description:

The rich, creamy texture of avocados come in part from its high content of anti-inflammatory monounsaturated fat. Avocados are also rich in the carotenoid lutein. Unlike most fruits, avocados are a good source of vitamin E, a micronutrient with anti-inflammatory effects. Diets high in these compounds are linked to decreased risk of the joint damage seen in early osteoarthritis.

Ingredients:

- 1 avocado
- 1/2 teaspoon minced garlic
- 1/2 teaspoon minced fresh ginger root
- 1 tablespoon olive oil

How to prepare:

- Stir together garlic, ginger, and olive oil; set aside for five minutes to allow the flavors to blend.
- Cut the avocado in half, and discard the pit; divide the sauce between the avocado halves.

Nutritional facts:
Calories: 164kcal, Fat: 15g, Carbs: 9.1g, Protein: 2.2g, Sodium: 157mg

14. Fresh Summer Organic Salsa

Description:

Avocados contain more than 25 vitamins, minerals, and phytonutrients. They have fiber, potassium, vitamin E, B-vitamins, and folic acid. Avocados are considered an excellent source of healthy fats when combined with a calorie-wise diet.

Ingredients:

- 2 tbsp organic olive oil
- 1 tbsp fresh lime juice
- 1/4 cup chopped cilantro
- 1/4 tsp unrefined sea salt
- 1/4 tsp freshly ground pepper
- 2 cups fresh organic corn, cut off the cob
- 2 avocados diced into 1/2 pieces
- 2 cups cherry tomatoes, quartered
- 1/4-1/2 cup finely diced red onion

How to prepare:

- In a large bowl, whisk together the olive oil, lime juice, cilantro, salt and pepper.
- Add to it the corn, avocado, cherry tomatoes and red onion.
- Stir gently and serve at room temperature.

Nutritional facts:

Calories: 206.2kcal, Fat: 15.1g, Carbs: 18.9g, Protein: 3.6g

15. Big Bang Fruit

Description:

Strawberries are naturally low in sugar and have more vitamin C per serving than an orange. Vitamin C can lower risk for gout, high blood pressure and cholesterol problems. Research has also shown that women who ate 16 or more strawberries a week had lower C-reactive protein (CRP), a measure of body-wide inflammation linked to arthritis flares and heart disease.

Ingredients:

- 2 avocados peeled and pitted chopped
- 1 cup strawberries finely chopped
- ½ of jalapeno minced, seeds removed
- 2 tbsp chopped cilantro
- ¼ tsp ground cinnamon
- 1 tbsp organic olive oil
- lime juice from ½ of a lime
- ¼ tsp unrefined sea salt

How to prepare:

- Mix all the ingredients together and gently stir.

Nutritional facts:

Calories: 226.8kcal, Fat: 18.8g, Carbs: 15.4g, Protein: 3.7g

16. Veggie Noodles

Description:
This pad Thai recipe is almost easier than calling for take-out. It's so fast and delicious. This meal would provide an excellent source of vitamins and nutrients.

Ingredients:

- 2 zucchini
- 1 carrot
- 2 green onion
- 1/2 cup mushrooms
- 1/2 cup cauliflower
- 1/2 cup mung bean sprouts
- 2 tablespoons sesame oil
- 1 tablespoon lemon juice
- 1 t garlic
- 1 t ginger

How to prepare:

- Use a spiralizer (or mandoline, or peeler) to create your noodles. Add in veggies of your choice then top with the sauce. It tastes even better after it sits to soak the flavors the next day.

Nutritional facts:
Calories: 369kcal, Fat: 14.4g, Carbs: 208g, Protein: 7.1g, Sodium: 957mg

17. Juicy Avocado

Description:

Avocados are thought to be effective at reducing pain and inflammation in people who suffer from osteoarthritis and gout.

Ingredients:

- 1 avocado - peeled, pitted and diced
- 1 lime, juiced
- 1 mango - peeled, seeded and diced
- 1 small red onion, chopped
- 1 habanero pepper, seeded and chopped
- 1 tablespoon chopped fresh cilantro

How to prepare:

- Place the avocado in a serving bowl, and mix with the lime juice.
- Mix in the mango, onion, habanero pepper, cilantro and salt.

Nutritional facts:
Calories: 252kcal, Fat: 15g, Carbs: 33g, Protein: 3g, Sodium: 204mg

18. Early Morning Salad

Description:
A simple spinach salad special by adding avocado, spices and fresh cilantro. Make it ahead, refrigerate and then toss right before serving.

Ingredients:

- 3 tablespoons fresh lime juice
- 3 tablespoons olive oil
- 1 tablespoon chopped fresh cilantro
- 1 teaspoon sugar
- 1/4 teaspoon ground cumin
- 1/4 teaspoon kosher salt
- 1/8 teaspoon black pepper
- 1 Hass avocado, peeled, pitted and thinly sliced
- 1 small red onion, thinly sliced
- 11 ounces baby spinach

How to prepare:

- Whisk lime juice, oil, cilantro, sugar, cumin, salt and pepper in a large serving bowl.
- Stir in avocado and red onion.
- Lay spinach on top. (Salad can be prepared and refrigerated up to 2 hours ahead.) Toss just before serving.

Nutritional facts:

Calories: 99kcal, Fat: 9g, Carbs: 5g, Sodium: 93mg

19. Garbanzos Soup

Description:
Whole grains lower levels of C-reactive protein (CRP) in the blood. CRP is a marker of inflammation associated with heart disease, diabetes and rheumatoid arthritis. Foods like oatmeal, brown rice and whole-grain cereals are excellent sources of whole grains.

Ingredients:

- 3 tablespoons olive oil
- 1 cup oats
- 5 large tomatoes, halved and sliced
- 1/3 cup onion, chopped
- 1 clove garlic, chopped
- 3 cups water, divided
- 1/2 bunch fresh cilantro
- 2 teaspoons chicken bouillon granules
- 1/2 teaspoon salt

How to prepare:

- Heat a large deep skillet or oven over medium-low heat. Pour in the olive oil, and let it heat up. Add the oats; cook and stir until toasted.
- In a blender or large food processor, combine the tomatoes, onion, garlic, 1 cup of water, and cilantro. Blend until smooth. Pour into the pan

with the toasted oats. Stir in the remaining 2 cups of water, and bring to a boil. Mix in the salt and chicken bouillon. Cover, and simmer for 15 minutes. Enjoy hot or warm.

Nutritional facts:
Calories: 218kcal, Fat: 12.1g, Carbs: 24.6g, Protein: 5.2g, Sodium: 493mg

20. Organic Guacamole

Description:

Avocados are the main ingredient in guacamole, a popular and healthy food commonly used as a sauce, spread or dip.

Ingredients:

- 2 avocados halved, pitted, and removed from peel
- ½ tsp salt
- ¼ tsp pepper
- ¼ cup fresh tomatoes, diced up
- ½ of a lime, juice squeezed out, about 1 tbsp
- 2 tbsp fresh cilantro, chopped
- 1 tbsp red onion (optional)

How to prepare:

- Combine all ingredients and mash with fork.
- Serve immediately.

Nutritional facts:
Calories: 148.9kcal, Fat: 13.4g, Carbs: 8.5g, Protein: 1.8g

21. Banana Oat Energy Bars

Description:

Bananas are simply a great food to consume overall, but especially if you're trying to do something about your arthritis. This vitamin mix includes folate, Vitamin C, and Vitamin B6, all of which help to battle back arthritis and keep your symptoms to a minimum.

Ingredients:

- 2 cups rolled oats
- 2 bananas, mashed
- 2 carrots, grated
- 1 apple, grated
- 1 cup unsweetened applesauce
- 1/2 cup chopped peanuts

How to prepare:

- Preheat oven to 350 degrees F (175 degrees C). Grease a 9x13-inch baking dish.
- Mix oats, bananas, carrots, apple, applesauce, and peanuts together in a bowl; spread into the prepared baking dish.
- Bake in the preheated oven until golden brown, about 20 minutes.

Nutritional facts:

Calories: 124kcal, Fat: 4g, Carbs: 20g, Protein: 3.6g, Sodium: 10mg

22. Breakfast Banana Green Smoothie

Description:

This smoothie is packed with nutrients and vitamins. It's also perfect if you're in a hurry to get to work. For people with arthritis, consuming a banana a day will not necessarily keep the doctor away, but it just might help minimize some of the severe symptoms of this potentially debilitating disease.

Ingredients:

- 2 cups baby spinach leaves, or to taste
- 1 banana
- 1 carrot, peeled and cut into large chunks
- 3/4 cup plain fat-free Greek yogurt, or to taste
- 3/4 cup ice

How to prepare:

- Put spinach, banana, carrot, yogurt, ice, and honey in a blender; blend until smooth.

Nutritional facts:
Calories: 367kcal, Fat: 0.8g, Carbs: 77.4g, Protein: 18.6g, Sodium: 168mg

23. Infused Olive Oil

Description:
Extra-virgin olive oil has benefits beyond stemming inflammation. Several studies have shown benefits for heart health, bone loss and neurological diseases.

Ingredients:

- 2 cups olive oil
- 1 teaspoon coarsely ground black pepper
- 1 tablespoon chopped fresh basil
- 1/2 teaspoon coarse sea salt
- 1 pinch crushed red pepper

How to prepare:

- In a medium bowl, mix together olive oil, coarsely ground black pepper, basil, coarse sea salt and red pepper. Cover and refrigerate the mixture. Allow it to sit approximately 1 hour before serving.

Nutritional facts:
Calories: 239kcal, Fat: 27g, Carbs: 0.1g, Sodium: 56mg

24. Happy Pistachos

Description:
Snack on pistachios to help with weight loss. Pistachios can also help lower LDL cholesterol and are high in potassium and antioxidants, including vitamins A and E and lutein – a compound also found in dark, leafy vegetables.

Ingredients:

- 2 cups shelled pistachios

How to prepare:

- Preheat oven to 350 degrees F.
- Spread the pistachios evenly on a rimmed cookie sheet. Place in the oven for about 6 to 8 minutes They will become very fragrant when they are done.
- Remove from oven and transfer to a plate immediately.
- If you want to remove the skins from the pistachios place them on a clean towel and rub them. The pieces will slide right off. It's easiest to do this when the pistachios are warm.
- Let the pistachios cool and then you can store them.

- They taste amazing in baking recipes when they are toasted.

Nutritional facts:
Calories: 170kcal, Fat: 14g, Carbs: 8g, Protein: 6g

25. Rosemary Walnuts

Description:

With their high ALA content, walnuts head the nut pack in omega-3 content, and researchers studying their effects have found they lower C-reactive protein (CRP), a marker of inflammation linked to increased risk of cardiovascular disease and arthritis. Eating walnuts regularly can lower cholesterol and reduce blood pressure.

Ingredients:

- 2 cups walnuts
- 2 cloves garlic, minced
- 1 tablespoon honey
- 1 tablespoon extra-virgin olive oil
- 1 tablespoon minced fresh rosemary
- 1 teaspoon salt

How to prepare:

- Preheat oven to 350 degrees F (175 degrees C). Line a baking sheet with parchment paper.
- Mix walnuts, garlic, honey, olive oil, rosemary, and salt together in a bowl until walnuts are coated; spread onto the prepared baking sheet.
- Bake in the preheated oven until walnuts are lightly browned, about 10 minutes.

Nutritional facts:

Calories: 188kcal, Fat: 8g, Carbs: 5.9g, Protein: 3.9g, Sodium: 291mg

26. Roasted Peanuts

Description:

Technically a legume, peanuts are the "nut" with the most protein. They're also cheaper than most nuts, so for people with arthritis trying to managing their weight, for example, they make a filling, inexpensive snack. Peanuts are also a good source of monounsaturated and polyunsaturated fats, and research shows adding them to your diet can help lower "bad" low-density lipoprotein (LDL) cholesterol and reduce heart disease risk. Peanuts deliver about 12% of your daily magnesium requirement, and may help keep blood sugar under control.

Ingredients:

- 1 pound raw peanuts, in shells

How to prepare:

- Preheat oven to 500 degrees F (260 degrees C).
- Arrange peanuts in a single layer on a cookie sheet, and place in the preheated oven.
- Turn oven off. Leave peanuts in oven for 1 hour without opening door. Serve warm or at room temperature.

Nutritional facts:
Calories: 322kcal, Fat: 27.9g, Carbs: 9.2g, Protein: 14.6g, Sodium: 10mg

27. Almond Carrots

Description:

Almonds are a good source of antioxidant vitamin E. Research suggests the monounsaturated fats from an almond-rich diet lower some markers of inflammation.

Ingredients:

- 2 pounds carrots, sliced
- 1 small onion, thinly sliced
- 1 small green bell pepper, cut into thin strips
- 1/2 cup vegetable oil
- 1/2 cup white sugar
- 1/4 cup distilled white vinegar
- 2 teaspoons almond extract
- 1 teaspoon dried basil

How to prepare:

- Boil carrots until tender but crisp. Remove from heat, drain, and place in a medium bowl with onion and pepper.
- In a medium saucepan over medium heat, blend oil, sugar, vinegar, almond extract and basil. Cook and stir until sugar is dissolved.
- Pour the oil mixture over the carrot mixture. Cover, and chill in the refrigerator 8 hours or overnight before serving cold.

Nutritional facts:

Calories: 145kcal, Fat: 9.4g, Carbs: 15.4g, Protein: 0.7g, Sodium: 44mg

28. No Bake Granola Bars

Description:

Flaxseed is one of the richest plant-based sources of the anti-inflammatory omega-3 fatty acid ALA. Studies show it may help lower overall and LDL cholesterol and reduce the complications of diabetes and heart disease risk. Crushing or milling the flaxseed make it easier for your body to digest.

Ingredients:

- 2 cups rolled oats
- 1 1/4 cups natural crunchy peanut butter
- 1 cup ground flaxseed
- 3/4 cup honey
- 3/4 cup dried cranberries
- 1/2 cup chocolate chips
- 1/4 cup sliced almonds

How to prepare:

- Stir oats, peanut butter, flaxseed, honey, cranberries, chocolate chips, and almonds together in a bowl;
- Refrigerate mixture at least 1 hour.
- Cut into 12 bars and wrap each individually in plastic wrap for storage.

Nutritional facts:

Calories: 391kcal, Fat: 21.3g, Carbs: 46.1g, Protein: 10.7g, Sodium: 136mg

29. Chia Seed Jam

Description:
Chia seeds are excellent source of anti-inflammatory, but their biggest benefit is probably their high fiber content. The fiber fills people up, which can help control weight.

Ingredients:

- 1/4 cup chia seeds
- 1/2 cup water
- 2 cups organic raspberries
- 1/2 cup organic blackberries
- 1/2 cup organic blueberries
- 2 organic strawberries, or more to taste
- 1/3 cup honey, or more to taste

How to prepare:

- Soak chia seeds in water until mixture has a jelly-like texture, about 5 minutes.
- Heat raspberries, blackberries, blueberries, strawberries, and honey in a saucepan over medium heat until berries are soft, about 15 minutes. Lightly crush berries with a fork or masher.
- Stir chia seed mixture into berry mixture. Remove from heat and let cool for at least 10 minutes.

Nutritional facts:

Calories: 70kcal, Fat: 1g, Carbs: 15.3g, Protein: 1g, Sodium: 2mg

30. Sardine Salsa

Description:
A 3-ounce serving of sardines contains about 1.4 grams of omega-3 fats and is a good source of vitamin D, which helps our bodies absorb calcium to build and maintain strong bones.

Ingredients:

- 1 avocado, mashed
- 2 romaine lettuce leaves, chopped
- 1/4 green bell pepper, finely chopped
- 1 teaspoon lemon juice
- 4 slices French bread
- 2 teaspoons extra-virgin olive oil
- 1 (4.375 ounce) sardines, drained
- 1 (14.5 ounce) tomatoes with basil, garlic, and oregano - drained

How to prepare:

- Preheat oven to 350 degrees F (175 degrees C).
- Combine avocado, chopped lettuce, chopped green pepper, and lemon juice in a small bowl.
- Brush extra-virgin olive oil on bread slices and toast in the preheated oven until browned, about 5 minutes on each side.

Nutritional facts:

Calories: 275kcal, Fat: 14.1g, Carbs: 26g, Protein: 12.9g, Sodium: 920mg

31. Cali Smoothie

Description:

Instead of squeezing the juice of fruits and vegetables, you are putting whole items in – giving you the added bonus of fiber, which helps clean out arteries and fight constipation. Colorful fruits and vegetables are also high in antioxidants. Adding berries or leafy greens like spinach or kale can give you big doses of vitamins and nutrients.

Ingredients:

- 7 large strawberries
- 1 (8 ounce) container lemon yogurt
- 1/3 cup orange juice

How to prepare:

- Place strawberries in a plastic container and freeze for about an hour.
- In a blender, combine strawberries, yogurt and orange juice. Blend until smooth. Pour into a tall glass and serve.

Nutritional facts:
Calories: 281kcal, Fat: 0.9g, Carbs: 57.4g, Protein: 12.9g, Sodium: 155mg

32. Vitabombs

Description:

Green beans act as an easy source for acquiring vitamins like A, C, K, B6, and folic acid. In terms of minerals, green beans are a good source of calcium, silicon, iron, manganese, potassium, and copper.

Ingredients:

- 1 1/2 pounds green beans, trimmed and cut into 2 inch pieces
- 1 1/2 cups water
- 1 tablespoon olive oil
- 1 tablespoon sugar
- 3/4 teaspoon garlic salt
- 1/4 teaspoon pepper
- 1 1/2 teaspoons chopped fresh basil
- 2 cups cherry tomato halves

How to prepare:

- Place beans and water in a large saucepan. Cover, and bring to a boil. Set heat to low, and simmer until tender, about 10 minutes. Drain off water, and set aside.
- Stir in sugar, garlic salt, pepper and basil. Add tomatoes, and cook stirring gently just until soft.

Pour the tomato mixture over the green beans, and toss gently to blend.

Nutritional facts:

Calories: 122kcal, Fat: 8g, Carbs: 12.6g, Protein: 2.6g, Sodium: 294mg

33. Veggie-Stars

Description:

Beetroot is your everyday superfood. They are a pretty pink nutritional powerhouse and an excellent example of how food can work as medicine. They are rich in folic acid, iron, magnesium, manganese and phosphorus.

Ingredients:

- 250g cooked beetroot dipped in vinegar (not pickled)
- 1 tin butterbeans (410g), drained & rinsed
- 1-2 cloves garlic, crushed
- Small bunch fresh chives, finely chopped (reserve a few for garnish)
- 3tbsp extra virgin olive oil
- Sea salt & freshly ground black pepper

How to prepare:

- Chop the beetroot into small dice, set aside in a medium bowl.
- In a food processor blitz the butterbeans with the garlic, chives and olive oil. Season to taste with sea salt & freshly ground black pepper.

Nutritional facts:
Calories: 180kcal, Fat: 16g, Carbs: 6g, Protein: 3g, Sodium: 880mg

34. Garlicky Kale

Description:

Besides being crowned as the "queen of greens", kale could also be referred to as the queen of Vitamin A. Compared to any other leafy green vegetable, kale has over 100 per cent of the average person's daily Vitamin A and C requirement. Kale is often compared to oranges because of its richness in vitamins.

Ingredients:

- 1 bunch kale
- 2 tablespoons olive oil
- 4 cloves garlic, minced

How to prepare:

- Tear the kale leaves into bite-size pieces from the thick stems; discard the stems.
- Heat the olive oil in a large pot over medium heat. Cook and stir the garlic in the hot oil until softened, about 2 minutes.
- Add the kale and continue cooking and stirring until the kale is bright green and wilted, about 5 minutes more.

Nutritional facts:
Calories: 120kcal, Fat: 7.5g, Carbs: 12.2g, Protein: 3.9g, Sodium: 49mg

35. Primal Cauliflower Steaks

Description:

Add some color to your cauliflower with turmeric. Several recent studies show that turmeric has anti-inflammatory properties and modifies immune system responses. These cauliflower steaks are easy to prepare and would make an excellent vegetarian side or main dish.

Ingredients:

- 1 large (about 1.2kg) cauliflower
- 1/4 cup extra virgin olive oil, plus extra for frying
- 1 teaspoon ground turmeric
- Fried curry leaves, to serve
- Thinly sliced fried red chilli, to serve

How to prepare:

- Preheat oven to 340F fan forced. Line 2 baking trays with foil.
- Cut the cauliflower into four 1.5cm-thick slices, leaving base intact. Cook steaks in extra virgin olive oil for 2-3 minutes each side or until golden.
- Whisk the olive oil with the turmeric in a bowl until combined. Brush over steaks.
- Roast cauliflower in the oven for 12-15 minutes or until tender and crisp.

Nutritional facts:

Calories: 161kcal, Fat: 15g, Carbs: 7g, Protein: 2.4g, Sodium: 30.8mg

36. Olive Dip

Description:

Though technically a fruit and not found in the produce aisle, olives and olive oil can be potent inflammation fighters. Olive contains compounds with anti-inflammatory properties. These compounds can dampen or switch off 100 inflammation causing genes.

Ingredients:

- 1 (4 ounce) can chopped green chiles, drained
- 1 onion, chopped
- 1 (5 ounce) jar green olives, chopped (reserve brine)
- 1 (6 ounce) can chopped black olives
- 1 1/2 cups shredded Cheddar cheese
- ground black pepper to taste
- garlic salt to taste
- 2 fresh red tomatoes, chopped

How to prepare:

- Chill a serving bowl in the freezer while you make the salsa.
- In a mixing bowl, combine the chopped green chiles, onion, green olives, and black olives.

- Lightly mix in the Cheddar cheese and tomatoes; season to taste with garlic salt and black pepper. If desired, mix in a little bit of the olive brine.
- Serve in the chilled bowl.

Nutritional facts:

Calories: 42kcal, Fat: 3.2g, Carbs: 1.9g, Protein: 1.8g, Sodium: 253mg

37. Round Veggie Chips

Description:
Oven-fried zucchini chips taste like they're fried, yet they are baked and amazingly crispy. These chips make a healthy substitute for french fries. Zucchini is rich in Vitamins A and C as well as antioxidants.

Ingredients:

- 3 small zucchini, sliced into ¼- inch rounds
- 2 tablespoons olive oil
- ½ cup Italian seasoned bread crumbs
- 2 tablespoons grated Parmesan cheese
- 2 teaspoons fresh oregano

How to prepare:

- Preheat oven to 350 degrees F (175 degrees C).
- Place zucchini in a bowl. Drizzle olive oil over zucchini and stir to coat; add bread crumbs and toss to coat. Spread coated zucchini onto a baking sheet. Sprinkle Parmesan cheese and oregano over coated zucchini.
- Bake in the preheated oven until zucchini are tender and cheese is browned, about 15 minutes

Nutritional facts:
Calories: 92kcal, Fat: 2g, Carbs: 14g, Protein: 6g, Sodium: 340mg

38. Kung-Fu Watercress

Description:

Iron is important in preventing anaemia and many people with arthritis are anaemic. Watercress is one of good sources of iron.

Ingredients:

- 1/2 cup chopped dried cranberries
- 1/4 cup red wine vinegar
- 1/4 cup balsamic vinegar
- 1 tablespoon minced garlic
- 1 1/4 teaspoons salt
- 1 cup extra virgin olive oil
- 6 bunches watercress - rinsed, dried and trimmed
- 3 bulbs fennel - trimmed, cored and thinly sliced
- 3 small heads radicchio, cored and chopped
- 1 cup pecan halves, toasted

How to prepare:

- In a bowl, combine the cranberries, red wine vinegar, balsamic vinegar, garlic and salt. Whisk in the olive oil.
- In a large salad bowl, combine the watercress, fennel, radicchio and pecans. Stir the vinaigrette and pour over salad. Toss well and serve at once.

Nutritional facts:

Calories: 178kcal, Fat: 15.4g, Carbs: 8.9g, Protein: 3.1g, Sodium: 202mg

39. OMG Oat

Description:

Omega-3 fatty acids are a key ingredient in helping to reduce the inflammation of arthritis and other joint problems, but getting enough of it every day can be challenging. This oatmeal tastes great and gets you half your daily requirements of omega-3s.

Ingredients:

- 1 cup rolled organic oats
- 1 cup filtered water
- 2 tbsp acidic medium (yogurt, lemon juice, apple cider vinegar, buttermilk)
- ½ tsp unrefined sea salt

How to prepare:

- Add 1 cup of oats, water, and the acidic medium into a glass bowl and stir well. Cover and let it sit overnight on the counter (at least 7-8 hours).
- In the morning add another 1 cup of filtered water and the unrefined sea salt, stir well.
- Heat to a low simmer and cook for 5 minutes.
- Serve with a generous portion of butter and cream.

Nutritional facts:

Calories: 153kcal, Fat: 3g, Carbs: 28.3g, Protein: 5.1g, Sodium: 202mg

40. Coconut Pumpkin Bread

Description:

Pumpkins are an excellent source of beta-cryptoxanthin, a powerful anti-inflammatory. This antioxidant is absorbed best when paired with a fat. Pumpkin skins are edible which makes preparing this bread very easy!

Ingredients:

- 4 eggs
- 3/4 cup canned organic pumpkin
- 1/4 cup coconut oil (melted and cooled)
- 1 tbsp raw honey
- 1/2 tsp unrefined sea salt
- 1/4 tsp baking soda
- 3/4 cup coconut flour
- 1 tsp cinnamon
- 1 tsp pumpkin spice

How to prepare:

- Blend together wet ingredients: eggs, pumpkin, cooled coconut oil, honey and mix well.
- In another bowl combine dry ingredients: salt, baking soda, coconut flour, cinnamon, pumpkin spice and shredded coconut.
- Combine wet and dry ingredients and stir until their are no more lumps.

- Pour into a greased bread pan and bake on 350 F for 40-45 minutes.

Nutritional facts:

Calories: 225.3kcal, Fat: 14g, Carbs: 14.4g, Protein: 7.3g

41. Raspberry Smoothie

Description:
Looking for a quick and easy breakfast which full of vitamin C? Try a smoothie. You can make this ahead of time and store it in the fridge. Just grab it and go before you head out the door. For lower sugar intake, use unsweetened yogurt.

Ingredients:

- 350g fresh raspberries
- 1 cup fresh strawberries, hulled, roughly chopped
- 1 1/2 cups (about 180g) natural yoghurt
- 1 cup milk

How to prepare:

- Place strawberries, raspberries, yoghurt, and milk in a blender. Blend until smooth. Pour into glasses. Serve.

Nutritional facts:
Calories: 160.3kcal, Fat: 4g, Carbs: 22g, Protein: 6g, Sodium: 65.83mg

42. Ginger's Secrets

Description:

Not only does ginger taste great in these quick and easy beverage, but it's also an excellent anti-inflammatory, helping to ease arthritis pain.

Ingredients:

- 1 cup chilled orange juice
- 1 cup chilled apple juice
- 2 tablespoons ginger beer cordial
- 1 tablespoon chopped fresh mint leaves
- 4 strawberries, hulled, roughly chopped
- 2 cups chilled lemonade
- ice cubes, to serve

How to prepare:

- Combine orange juice, apple juice and cordial in a large bowl. Top with mint, strawberries, lemonade and ice. Stir to combine. Serve.

Nutritional facts:
Calories: 95kcal, Carbs: 22g, Protein: 1g, Sodium: 28.3mg

43. Cranberry Sauce

Description:

> Cranberry juice is able to block this bacteria from growing and multiplying; researchers believe that patients in the early stages of rheumatoid arthritis can benefit from a high intake of cranberry juice.

Ingredients:

- 12 ounces cranberries
- 1 cup white sugar
- 1 cup orange juice

How to prepare:

- In a medium sized saucepan over medium heat, dissolve the sugar in the orange juice. Stir in the cranberries and cook until the cranberries start to pop (about 10 minutes). Remove from heat and place sauce in a bowl. Cranberry sauce will thicken as it cools.

Nutritional facts:
Calories : 95kcal, Fat : 14g, Carbs : 24g, Protein : 7.3g

44. Honey Yummy Pineapple

Description:

Pineapple contains immune-boosting vitamin C. It also provides a key enzyme called bromelain, which is chock-full of anti-inflammatory substances that can help reduce joint swelling linked to rheumatoid arthritis.

Ingredients:

- 4 slices fresh pineapple
- 2 tablespoons honey
- 1 teaspoon lemon juice

How to prepare:

- To Marinate: Combine honey, brandy and lemon juice in a nonporous glass dish or bowl. Mix together and add pineapple; coat well with marinade mixture. Cover dish and marinate in refrigerator for 1 hour.
- Preheat grill to medium heat and lightly oil grate.
- Remove pineapple from dish or bowl, discarding any leftover marinade. Place pineapple wedges directly on rack or in a basket and grill for about 10 minutes, turning, until pineapple is hot and caramelized.

Nutritional Facts:

Calories : 59kcal, Fat : 0.1, Carbs : 11.8g, Protein : 0.3g

45. Senor Pineapple

Description:

Pineapple is rich in magnesium, manganese and a vital enzyme known as bromelain. It also contains copper, potassium, vitamin B1, vitamin B6, dietary fibre, folate and pantothenic acid.

Ingredients:

- 1 cup brown sugar
- 2 teaspoons ground cinnamon
- 1 pineapple - peeled, cored, and cut into 6 wedges

How to prepare:

- Preheat an outdoor grill for medium-high heat and lightly oil the grate.
- Whisk brown sugar and cinnamon together in a bowl. Pour sugar mixture into a large resealable plastic bag. Place pineapple wedges in bag and shake to coat each wedge.
- Grill pineapple wedges on the preheated grill until heated through, 3 to 5 minutes per side.

Nutritional facts:
Calories : 225kcal, Fat : 0.3g, Carbs :66g, Protein :1.3g, Sodium :13mg

46. Dinner Bass

Description:

Eating more than one serving of all types of fish every week for a minimum of 10 years will reduce the risk of arthritis by 29%!

Ingredients:

- 1 lemon, juiced
- 3 tablespoons olive oil
- 2 tablespoons chopped fresh parsley
- 1 pinch crushed red pepper flakes
- 1 pinch salt
- 1 pound skinless wild striped bass fillets

How to prepare:

- Whisk together lemon juice, olive oil, parsley, pepper flakes, and salt in a bowl. Add bass fillets; marinate for 10 minutes.
- Preheat an outdoor grill for medium-high heat and lightly oil the grate.
- Grill bass on the preheated grill until fish flakes easily with a fork, about 5 minutes each side. Discard any remaining marinade.

Nutritional facts:

Calories : 226kcal, Fat: 15.5g, Carbs: 3.1g, Protein: 21.8g, Sodium: 179mg

47. Legacy of Pear

Description:

One pear contains up to 11 percent of our daily recommended intake of vitamin C and 9.5 percent of our daily recommended intake of copper. Pears are also said to have more nutrients per calorie than calorie per nutrient.

Ingredients:

- 1 ripe pear - peeled, cored, and chopped
- 1/2 cup white wine
- 1 clove garlic, chopped
- 2 teaspoons Dijon mustard
- 1/4 cup white balsamic vinegar
- 1 teaspoon ground black pepper
- 1/4 teaspoon sea salt
- 1/2 cup olive oil

How to prepare:

- Blend the pear, white wine, garlic, Dijon mustard, white balsamic vinegar, black pepper, and sea salt in a blender until well combined; drizzle the olive oil into the mixture in a thin, steady stream while continuing to blend. Blend a few seconds longer until the salad dressing is thick and creamy.

Nutritional facts:

Calories : 101kcal, Fat : 9g, Carbs : 3.6g, Protein : 0.1g, Sodium : 60mg

48. Japanese pickled ginger

Description:
Do you keep ginger in your spice cabinet? Maybe it should be in your medicine cabinet. Besides being a tasty spice often used to enhance holiday treats, ginger can soothe upset stomachs and diminish nausea, and studies show it may help pain and inflammation, too.

Ingredients:

- 125g fresh ginger, peeled
- 1 teaspoon salt
- 60ml (1/4 cup) rice wine vinegar
- 60ml (1/4 cup) water
- 55g (1/4 cup) caster sugar

How to prepare:

- Slice the ginger into thin strips. Transfer to a bowl and sprinkle with salt. Stir until well combined. Set aside for 30 minutes to allow the salt to extract excess liquid.
- Stir the rice wine vinegar, water and sugar in a small saucepan over medium heat until the sugar dissolves. Increase heat to high. Bring to the boil. Pour the vinegar mixture over ginger. Set aside for 5 minutes to cool slightly. Seal and place in the fridge for 24 hours to develop the flavours.

Nutritional facts:

Calories: 16kcal, Carbs :3.5g

49. Sparkle of Watermelon & Ginger

Description:
The anti-inflammatory properties help relieve pain and improve function for all types of arthritis. Mix ginger and watermelon together and make a good use of them.

Ingredients:

- 1kg piece seedless watermelon, skin removed, cut into chunks
- 2 cups ice cubes
- 1/4 cup fresh mint leaves
- 2 tablespoons caster sugar
- 1 teaspoon finely grated fresh ginger

How to prepare:

- Place watermelon in a blender. Blend until finely chopped. Add ice, mint leaves, sugar and ginger. Blend until ice is crushed.
- Pour into serving glasses and serve immediately.

Nutritional facts:
Calories : 114kcal, Fat : 1g, Carbs : 24g, Protein : 1g, Sodium : 5.31mg

50. Pickled Onion

Description:
Onions are low in calories, have virtually no fat and are loaded with healthful components that fight inflammation in arthritis and related conditions. One flavonoid found in onions, called quercetin, has been shown to inhibit inflammation.

Ingredients:

- 1 red onion, chopped
- 1/2 cup red wine vinegar
- 3 tablespoons distilled white vinegar
- 1 1/2 tablespoons salt
- 1 teaspoons white sugar

How to prepare:

- Bring the onion, red wine vinegar, white vinegar, salt, and sugar to a boil in a saucepan over medium-high heat. Remove from heat and allow mixture to steep until the onion is tender, about 20 minutes.

Nutritional facts:
Calories : 19kcal, Fat : 0g, Carbs : 4.5g, Protein : 0.2g, Sodium : 1745mg

51. Two-tone Granitas

Description:
How to make a cool dessert in the hot summer and be healthy with your arthritis pain? Let's beat the heat and pain with this sweet grape granita.

Ingredients:

- 500g red grapes, picked
- 500g green grapes, picked
- 750ml (3 cups) water
- 270g (1/4 cups) caster sugar

How to prepare:

- Place the red grapes in the jug of a blender and blend until pureed. Pour through a fine sieve into a medium bowl, gently pressing with the back of a spoon to extract as much liquid as possible. Discard the skins and seeds. Repeat with green grapes.
- Combine the water and sugar in a saucepan over low heat. Cook, stirring, for 2-3 minutes or until sugar dissolves. Increase heat to medium-high and bring to a simmer. Simmer for 8-10 minutes or until syrup thickens slightly. Remove from heat and set aside for 10 minutes to cool.

- Add half the sugar mixture to the red grape juice and remaining sugar mixture to green grape juice. Pour into separate airtight containers and cover with lids. Place in the freezer for 3-4 hours or until ice crystals form around the edges. Use a fork to roughly break up the frozen grape juice. Cover and return to the freezer for a further 8 hours or until completely set.
- Use a fork to scrape the granitas into coarse crystals. Cover and return to the freezer for a further 1 hour.
- Divide the red grape granita and green grape granita among serving glasses and serve immediately.

Nutritional facts:
Calories : 455kcal, Carbs: 107g, Protein: 2g, Sodium : 10.5mg

52. Kiwi Cooler

Description:
Research suggests that people who eat a diet low in vitamin C may have a greater risk of developing some kinds of arthritis. Kiwi is one of vitamin C-rich foods!

Ingredients:

- 1/2 cup (110g) caster sugar
- 1/2 cup (125ml) boiling water
- 4 gold and 4 green kiwi fruit
- 1/3 cup (80ml) lime juice (from 3-4 limes)
- 1/2 cup mint leaves
- 2 cups ice cubes
- 1 cup (250ml) sparkling water

How to prepare:

- In a large jug, dissolve 1/2 cup (110g) caster sugar in 1/2 cup (125ml) boiling water, then place in an ice bath or fridge to chill. Peel and roughly chop 4 gold and 4 green kiwi fruit, then blend until smooth with the cooled syrup, 1/3 cup (80ml) lime juice, 1/2 firmly packed cup mint leaves and 2 cups ice cubes. Pour into a jug and top up with 1 cup (250ml) sparkling water, or divide among glasses and top up with wine or water. Serve with extra mint.

Nutritional facts:

Calories: 92kcal, Carbs: 18g, Protein: 1g, Sodium: 9.6mg

53. Kiwifruit Break

Description:
Eat some kiwi and get vitamin C in your breakfast. Time to start a new day!

Ingredients:

- 4 kiwifruit, peeled, chopped
- 1 red capsicum, halved, seeded, cut into 1cm pieces
- 2 shallots, ends trimmed, thinly sliced
- 1/3 cup fresh coriander, chopped
- 2 teaspoons fresh lime juice

How to prepare:

- Place the kiwifruit, capsicum, shallot, coriander and lime juice in a glass or ceramic bowl. Season with salt and pepper. Stir gently until well combined.

Nutritional facts:
Calories: 56kcal, Fat: 0.5g, Carbs: 11g, Protein: 2g

54. Mexican Bean Soup

Description:

Beans are loaded with fiber and phytonutrients, which help lower CRP, an indicator of inflammation found in the blood. Beans are also an excellent and inexpensive source of protein, with about 15 grams per cup, which is important for muscle health.

Ingredients:

- 1 tablespoon olive oil
- 1 onion, chopped
- 1 clove garlic, crushed
- 2 1/2 cups organic chicken stock
- 400g tomato pieces
- 2 tablespoons tomato paste
- 420g beans, drained
- 1 small red capsicum, chopped
- 1 small green capsicum, chopped
- 1 teaspoon Mexican seasoning
- fresh basil leaves, to serve

How to prepare:

- Place oil, onion, and garlic in a large saucepan over medium-high heat. Cook, stirring, for 1 to 2 minutes or until soft.

- Add stock, tomato and tomato paste. Bring to the boil. Simmer for 10 minutes.
- Add beans, capsicum and seasoning. Cook for 5 minutes. Season with salt and pepper. Ladle into bowls and top with fresh basil leaves.

Nutritional facts:
Calories: 742kcal, Fat: 6g, Carbs: 20g, Protein: 8g, Sodium: 1155mg

55. Afternoon Soup

Description:

Carrot get its distinctive color from carotenoids like beta-cryptoxanthin. Eating food rich in beta-cryptoxanthin could reduce your risk of developing RA and other inflammatory conditions.

Ingredients:

- 1 tablespoon olive oil
- 1 leek, halved lengthways, thinly sliced
- 6 carrots, peeled, chopped
- 4cm piece ginger, peeled, grated
- 2 cups salt-reduced vegetable stock
- 2 cups water
- Light sour cream, to serve
- Fresh dill, to serve
- Toast, to serve

How to prepare:

- Heat oil in a large saucepan over medium heat. Add leek, carrots and ginger. Cook, uncovered, stirring occasionally, for 8 minutes, or until vegetables start to soften.
- Add stock and water to saucepan. Cover. Bring to the boil. Reduce heat to medium-low. Simmer,

- covered, for 20 minutes, or until carrots are very tender.
- Remove from heat. Set aside to cool slightly. Process or blend soup until smooth. Return to saucepan. Heat with medium-high heat until hot. Season with salt and pepper.
- Ladle soup into bowls. Top with sour cream and dill. Serve with toast.

Nutritional facts:
Calories: 97kcal, Fat: 5g, Carbs: 8g, Protein: 2g, Sodium: 520mg

ADDITIONAL TITLES FROM THIS AUTHOR

70 Effective Meal Recipes to Prevent and Solve Being Overweight: Burn Fat Fast by Using Proper Dieting and Smart Nutrition

By

Joe Correa CSN

48 Acne Solving Meal Recipes: The Fast and Natural Path to Fixing Your Acne Problems in Less Than 10 Days!

By

Joe Correa CSN

41 Alzheimer's Preventing Meal Recipes: Reduce or Eliminate Your Alzheimer's Condition in 30 Days or Less!

By

Joe Correa CSN

70 Effective Breast Cancer Meal Recipes: Prevent and Fight Breast Cancer with Smart Nutrition and Powerful Foods

By

Joe Correa CSN

www.ingramcontent.com/pod-product-compliance
Lightning Source LLC
Chambersburg PA
CBHW070156080526
44586CB00015B/2021